The Prosperous Path

Achieving Financial Success
&
Inner Peace

By Laura Henry-Pugh

ISBN: 9798392453085

Contact Information

Website: lhpventures.com

Email Address: laura@lhpventures.com

Dedication

To those who have trouble living in the material world to balance money and faith, I hope this book gives you insight and confidence to achieve financial success.

Thank You...

for purchasing this book. As my gift to you, please visit LHPVentures.com/prosperouspath to get access to our **FREE** digital journal designed specifically for this book.

Also, don't forget to leave a review on Amazon.

Table of Contents

Introduction..1

Chapter 1: The Connection between Financial Success and
            Inner Peace...3

Chapter 2: How Our Thoughts & Beliefs Affect Our

            Finances 8

Chapter 3: Creating a Roadmap to Prosperity 13

Chapter 4: How to Make Conscious Choices

            with Your Money.......................................19

Chapter 5: Strategies for Savings and Investment...........25

Chapter 6: Managing Debt and Building Credit................31

Chapter 7: Overcoming Financial Stress and Anxiety 43

Chapter 8: How to Find Inner Peace in a Material World..59

Chapter 9: Prioritizing Wellness and Happiness...............69

Chapter 10: The Path to Sustainable Prosperity and

            Inner Peace 81

Appendix...83

Introduction

It can be challenging to balance financial prosperity and inner peace in a world where we are incessantly bombarded with messages about what success entails and to what we should aspire. The notion that accumulating wealth and possessions is the key to happiness was ingrained in many of us through conditioning.

The Prosperous Path: Achieving Financial Success and Inner Peace is a book that explores the interconnectedness of financial success, inner peace, and overall wellness. It offers practical strategies for managing finances, reducing stress, and finding a sense of inner calm amidst the chaos of daily life.

This book is not just about money but our relationship with money and how it impacts every aspect of our lives. It provides a spiritual perspective on wealth and prosperity. It shows how incorporating mindfulness and gratitude into our financial practices can lead to greater abundance and fulfillment.

Through a combination of personal anecdotes, practical advice, and biblical wisdom, this book aims to empower readers to take control of their finances and find a sense of peace and contentment that transcends material possessions.

The Prosperous Path is for anyone who is seeking to live a more balanced and fulfilling life, free from the stress and anxiety that often accompany financial insecurity. Regardless of whether you are at the beginning of your financial journey or seeking to strengthen your spiritual relationship with money and wealth, this book provides assistance and encouragement throughout the process.

I hope this book will inspire and encourage you to discover your own path to financial success and inner peace and that it will serve as a valuable resource on your journey toward a more prosperous and fulfilling life.

Chapter One

The Connection Between Financial Success and Inner Peace

Financial success and inner peace are two seemingly disparate goals, but they are more interconnected than one might think. The pursuit of financial success often creates stress, anxiety, and dissatisfaction. At the same time, inner peace is often seen as something that can only be achieved through spiritual or philosophical practices unrelated to finances. However, the truth is that financial success and inner peace are intricately linked, and one can greatly enhance the other.

Financial success, while important, can only provide temporary happiness and satisfaction if it is not accompanied by inner peace. Money can buy material comforts, but it cannot buy true happiness or contentment. On the other hand, inner peace can provide a sense of calm and satisfaction, but it is difficult to maintain if one is constantly struggling with financial stress.

The connection between financial success and inner peace lies in how we approach our finances. When we understand the psychological and spiritual aspects of money and make conscious choices about our spending and saving, we can align our financial goals with our values and find peace and satisfaction in both our financial and personal lives. This book explores the relationship between financial success and inner peace and provides practical strategies for achieving both.

In the following story, you will see how Mike changed his life to find inner peace.

A man named Mike was at a crossroads in his life. He had just graduated from college and was unsure about what career path to take. He had been applying for several jobs but had not received any offers.

One day, while Mike was sitting in his living room, feeling overwhelmed and anxious about his future, his grandfather came over to visit. Grandpa Joe was a wise and kind man who always knew just what to say to make Mike feel better.

As they talked, Mike shared his worries and fears with his grandpa.

Grandpa listened patiently, then took out his Bible and turned to Proverbs 3:5-6. He read the scripture out loud, "Trust in the Lord with all your heart and lean not on your own understanding; in all your ways submit to him, and he will make your paths straight." He told Mike it was a reminder to trust God's plan, even when things seemed uncertain.

Mike was inspired by his grandpa's words and took them to heart. He started to pray and ask for guidance, and he also began to network and reach out to people in his field of interest.

One day, Mike received a call from the company to which he had applied. His resume impressed them, and they asked him to come in for an interview. After a few interviews, they offered him the job, and he was thrilled to accept.

Trust in the Lord with all your heart and lean not on your own understanding; in all your ways submit to him, and he will make your paths straight. – Proverbs 3:5-6

Reflections

What does financial success mean to you, and why is it important?

_____

_____

_____

_____

_____

_____

_____

_____

_____

_____

Reflections

What role does spirituality or faith play in your approach to finances, if any?

_____

_____

_____

_____

_____

_____

_____

_____

_____

_____

_____

The goal isn't more money. The goal is living life on your terms.

Chris Brogan — Author, Journalist

Chapter Two

How Our Thoughts and Beliefs Affect Our Finances

Money is more than just currency; it symbolizes power, security, and success. Our thoughts and beliefs about money can significantly impact our financial well-being. Negative thoughts and beliefs, such as feelings of insecurity or a lack of self-worth, can lead to unhealthy financial habits, such as overspending or hoarding, and prevent us from reaching our financial goals.

Conversely, positive thoughts and beliefs about money can lead to healthy financial practices and success. This can include a belief in abundance, a focus on gratitude, and understanding the value of hard work and careful planning.

It is important to examine our own beliefs and attitudes about money and work towards developing a positive and empowered relationship with it. This can involve challenging limiting beliefs and negative thought patterns and practicing mindfulness and gratitude regarding our finances. By understanding the psychology of money and the role that our thoughts and beliefs play, we can take control of our financial lives and work towards financial success and inner peace.

Much of our beliefs around money came from our parents, grandparents, or other significant family members and friends. Not all of it was positive. Here is an example:

A little girl named Lily loved to play and explore the world around her. One day, while playing in her parents' living room, she accidentally knocked over a vase that shattered into a million pieces. Her parents were furious and scolded her for being so careless. Lily felt ashamed and guilty, even though it was just an accident.

Years later, as an adult, Lily found that she tended to overspend and accumulate debt. She realized that her childhood experience of being shamed for a mistake had made her feel unworthy and inadequate. She tried to fill the void with material possessions, hoping they would make her feel better about herself.

But then, one day, a friend of Lily's explained that she needed to make wiser decisions concerning her money. After speaking with her friend, she sought counsel to help her make wise choices.

Lily focused away from material possessions and toward a deeper connection with God. She found that as she trusted Him more and put God first, she recognized that financial success could come as a result of faithfulness and hard work. She experienced a sense of inner peace and contentment that no amount of money or possessions could provide.

In the end, Lily realized that her childhood experience of breaking the vase had taught her a valuable lesson about the dangers of attaching too much importance to material things. It had taken her some time, but she finally found her way back to the truth that true wealth and happiness come from a deep and abiding trust in God.

We need to have an open mind and be willing to take a shift in our beliefs about money. Many people may have difficulty achieving financial success due to their religious background. Understand that God wants us to live a prosperous life. God will provide, but we must meet God halfway. We must plan our finances and trust the Lord to deliver our needs and wants.

"His master replied, 'Well done, good and faithful servant! You have been faithful with a few things; I will put you in charge of many things. Come and share your master's happiness!' – Matthew 25:21

Reflections

What are your earliest memories of money?

_____

_____

_____

_____

_____

_____

_____

_____

_____

_____

Reflections

How have they influenced your beliefs and habits around money?

_____

_____

_____

_____

_____

_____

_____

_____

_____

_____

A good financial plan is a road map that shows us exactly how the choices we make today will affect our future."

Alexa Von Tobel, CEO LearnVe

Chapter Three

Creating a Roadmap to Prosperity

One of the key steps toward financial success and inner peace is setting clear financial goals and priorities. This step involves taking a deep look at your current financial situation, identifying what is important to you, and creating a roadmap for how you will achieve your financial goals.

When setting financial goals, it is essential to be specific, realistic, and measurable. This means setting goals that are attainable within a specific time frame and that are specific enough to give you a clear understanding of what success looks like. Additionally, it would be best if you prioritized your goals based on what is most important to you and what will bring you the greatest sense of financial stability and security.

Follow the steps below:

1. **Determine your current financial situation:** Assess your income, expenses, debts, and savings to understand your current financial situation.

2. **Identify your financial priorities:**
   Decide what you want to achieve financially, whether paying off debt, save for retirement, or buying a house.

3. **Make your goals specific:**
   Clearly define what you want to achieve, when you want to achieve it, and how much you want to save or earn.

4. **Make your goals realistic:**
   Consider your current financial situation, income, and expenses to determine if your goals are achievable.

5. **Make your goals measurable:**
   Assign a specific amount of money to each purpose and set a deadline for achieving it.

6. **Create a plan of action:**
   Develop a plan to reach your financial goals, including budgeting, saving, and investing.

7. **Track your progress:**
   Regularly review your financial situation and monitor your progress toward your goals to ensure you are on track.

8. **Adjust your plan as needed:**
   If you encounter obstacles or your financial situation changes, adjust your strategy to keep your goals attainable.

In order to ensure that your goals are achievable, it is also important to create a budget and stick to it. This involves tracking your expenses, identifying areas where you can cut back, and ensuring you save enough each month to reach your financial goals.

Setting clear financial goals and priorities and following a budget can create a roadmap to financial success and inner peace. This budget will give you a sense of control and empowerment regarding your finances and help you avoid feelings of stress and anxiety.

Here is an example of a man who was diligently planning his finances.

A young man named Jack had always dreamed of starting his own business. He knew it would take hard work and dedication, but he was willing to do whatever it took to achieve his goals.

At first, Jack was so eager to get started that he rushed into things without proper planning or preparation. He thought success would come quickly and easily if he just put in the effort. But soon enough, he realized that he was struggling to get ahead.

One day, Jack spoke to a successful entrepreneur who gave him valuable advice. The entrepreneur told Jack that diligence and careful planning were key to success. He explained that rushing into things without proper preparation was a surefire way to fail, while taking the time to plan and strategize would help him achieve his goals.

Jack took this advice to heart and decided to slow down and focus on planning his business carefully. He spent weeks researching his industry, studying his competition, and setting achievable goals. He knew that success wouldn't come overnight, but he was willing to put in the work.

As time went on, Jack faced many challenges and setbacks. But he refused to give up. He stayed committed to his goals and continued to put in the work, day in and day out.

Years later, Jack's business was thriving. He had built a successful company that provided jobs for dozens of people in his community. Looking back, he knew the key to his success was the diligence and careful planning he had put in from the beginning.

The lesson here is simple: success requires hard work, dedication, and careful planning. It's essential to take the time to strategize and prepare for your goals rather than rushing into things blindly. So, if you're feeling overwhelmed or discouraged, remember that success is possible if you stay committed and put in the work.

> The craving of a sluggard will be the death of him, because his hands refuse to work. - Proverbs 21:5

Reflections

What is your current financial situation?

_____

_____

_____

_____

_____

_____

_____

_____

_____

_____

Reflections

What are your financial priorities?

_____

_____

_____

_____

_____

_____

_____

_____

_____

_____

_____

_____

Chapter 4

How to Make Conscious Choices with Your Money

Mindful spending involves being intentional and deliberate about using your money and making choices that align with your values, goals, and priorities. It is about making purchases that bring you joy and satisfaction rather than just trying to keep up with the latest trends or accruing more possessions.

The initial step towards practicing mindful spending is to grasp your values, objectives, and priorities and employ them as a framework for your spending choices. This might involve asking yourself: Is this purchase aligned with my values and goals? Do I really need this, or can I live without it? How will this purchase impact my financial situation in the long run?

- **What are your core values?**
  Core values are a deeply internalized philosophical guide that profoundly influences goal setting, decision-making, conflict resolution, and one's life.

- **What are your financial goals?**

  Financial goals are specific objectives that you set for your personal finances. These objectives can be short-term or long-term and can be related to saving money, reducing debt, or investing for the future.

For example, if you are in a store and see something you like or want before purchasing, look at it again and decide if this will help you reach your financial goal. Is it part of your core values and beliefs? If it isn't, pass it by. If you do this with every purchase, you will be more conscious of your decisions about your spending habits.

In addition to making conscious spending decisions, it is also necessary to understand the underlying emotions and motivations behind your spending habits. For example, are you spending money to cope with stress or boredom? Or are you trying to fill an emotional void with material possessions? By becoming more aware of the reasons behind your spending habits, you can learn to make more mindful choices with your money. Many of these behaviors stem from childhood and how you learned about money.

Let me tell you about Betty.

Betty had a good job, a loving family, and many friends. Still, she couldn't shake off the constant feeling of boredom and anxiety that plagued her. Betty tried everything to cope, from meditation to exercise, but nothing seemed to work. Eventually, she discovered the perfect solution to her problems: shopping.

Whenever Betty felt anxious or bored, she would browse the nearest shopping center. She would wander from store to store, trying on clothes and shoes and buying anything that caught her eye. At first, it seemed harmless, but Betty's shopping habit started spiraling out of control as time passed.

Before long, Betty spent more money than she could afford on clothes, shoes, accessories, and other frivolous items. She bought things she didn't need and would never use to get that fleeting rush of excitement and pleasure. Her credit card bills started accumulating, and she felt more anxious than ever.

One day, Betty decided to seek help for her problem. She went to see a therapist who specialized in anxiety and addiction. The therapist patiently listened as Betty described her shopping habits and the problems they caused in her life.

"Betty," the therapist said, "I think you're using shopping to avoid dealing with your anxiety and boredom. It's a distraction, but it's not a solution. You need to find healthier ways to cope with your feelings."

Betty felt a wave of relief wash over her. She had never thought about her shopping habit in that way before. She realized she had avoided her feelings instead of dealing with them.

With the therapist's help, Betty began to explore new ways of coping with her anxiety and boredom. She practiced yoga and meditation, started painting, and even tried cooking. Slowly but surely, she began to feel better. She realized there were healthier, more fulfilling ways to deal with her feelings than shopping.

In the end, Betty learned that true happiness and contentment come from within, not from material possessions. She still enjoyed shopping occasionally, but now she did it in moderation and never as a way to cope with her feelings. And whenever she felt anxious or bored, she knew she could turn to her new hobbies and coping strategies instead.

By practicing mindful spending, you can build a healthier relationship with your money and enjoy a greater sense of inner peace and fulfillment, knowing that your spending decisions align with your values, goals, and priorities.

> Then he said to them, "Watch out! Be on your guard against all kinds of greed; life does not consist in an abundance of possessions."
> - Luke 12:15

Reflections

What are some of the emotional triggers that lead you to spend money impulsively?

_____

_____

_____

_____

_____

_____

_____

_____

_____

_____

_____

Reflections

Can you think of a time when you made an impulsive purchase that you regretted later? What could you have done differently?

_____

_____

_____

_____

_____

_____

_____

_____

_____

_____

_____

_____

Chapter 5

Strategies for Savings and Investment

Building a strong financial foundation is critical for achieving financial success and inner peace. This involves creating and maintaining a balanced budget, reducing debt, and establishing a solid savings and investment plan.

When it comes to savings, it is vital to start by setting aside a portion of your monthly income, even if it is just a small amount. This allows you to save for short-term goals.

- **Build an emergency fund**. This fund should be large enough to cover at least three to six months of living expenses.

- **Unexpected events**. Would include job loss or medical emergencies.

In addition to saving for emergencies, it is also important to save for long-term goals.

- **Build a retirement plan.**

- **Education expenses.**

- **Purchase a home or vehicle.**

Savings can be made through employer-sponsored retirement plans like 401(k)s and individual retirement accounts (IRAs), as well as other savings vehicles like savings accounts, certificates of deposit, and investment accounts.

When it comes to investment, it is crucial to educate yourself on the different types of investments available and to choose investments that align with your financial goals, risk tolerance, and time horizon Investments might include a mix of stocks, bonds, real estate, and other alternative investments.

It is also effective to have a diversified portfolio, which means spreading your investments across different assets and industries, to reduce risk. Additionally, it is crucial to regularly review your investments and adjust, as needed, based on changes in your financial situation, goals, and market conditions.

Building a strong financial foundation can create a solid platform for future financial success and inner peace. This will give you the peace of mind and security to focus on other aspects of your life, and to live with a sense of abundance and gratitude, knowing that you are well-prepared for the future.

In my book, *Family Financial Freedom: A Beginner's Guide to Money Management*, I detail the different types of financial portfolios. book also guides you to review your current accounts and the options you can consider.

What does it mean to have a solid financial foundation?

There was a man named Max, a hardworking, blue-collar worker who dreamed of owning his own construction company. He spent years saving up his hard-earned money and finally had enough to start his own business.

Excited to start his journey, Max began to lay the foundation for his company. He bought equipment, hired a team, and started taking on projects. But soon, he realized that he had not considered all the costs of running a successful construction company.

He struggled to manage his finances and found himself falling behind on payments. As a result, his team started to lose faith in him, and he risked losing everything he had worked so hard for.

But Max was not one to give up easily. He knew that if he wanted to succeed, he had to sit down and count the cost. He had to re-evaluate his business plan and make some tough decisions.

With renewed focus and determination, Max started to turn things around. He cut back on unnecessary expenses, renegotiated contracts, and ensured his team was motivated and on track.

Slowly, Max's business started to flourish. His reputation grew, and he began taking on bigger, more challenging projects. He continued to count the cost, never losing sight of his ultimate goal.

Years later, Max looked back on his journey with pride. He knew that he had built something truly remarkable that had started with a dream and grew into a successful business.

Overall, Max had been bold and determined, and in the end, he triumphed. Max's story inspires all who dream of building something of their own. With hard work and determination, anything is possible.

"Suppose one of you wants to build a tower. Won't you first sit down and estimate the cost to see if you have enough money to complete it? For if you lay the foundation and are not able to finish it, everyone who sees it will ridicule you, saying, 'This person began to build and wasn't able to finish'. - Luke 14:28-30

Reflections

What are your short-term financial goals, and how are you currently saving for them?

_____

_____

_____

_____

_____

_____

_____

_____

_____

_____

_____

Reflections

What long-term financial goals do you have, and how are you planning to save for them?

_____

_____

_____

_____

_____

_____

_____

_____

_____

_____

_____

Chapter 6

Managing Debt and Building Credit

Debt can be a major source of stress and a barrier to financial success and inner peace. It is imperative to understand your debt types, how it affects your finances, and what steps you can take to reduce or eliminate them.

There are two main types of debt: good debt and bad debt. Good debt includes investments in assets like education, homes, and businesses that will likely increase in value over time and can provide long-term financial benefits. Bad debt, on the other hand, includes high-interest consumer debt like credit card balances and personal loans that do not offer any long-term benefits.

Even though education is considered a good debt, you should not be so in debt that it takes years to pay off. According to recent data from the Federal Reserve, the median time it takes for borrowers to repay their student loan debt fully is about 17 years. However, this figure can be significantly shorter or longer depending on the individual's circumstances.[i]

Begin to save early for your children's or grandchildren's educational expenses and include inflation over the years until the child reaches 18.

Prioritizing bad debt repayment as soon as feasible while continuing to meet the minimum payments on good debt is crucial to effectively managing debt and minimizing stress. This can be done through various strategies, such as consolidating debt, negotiating with creditors for lower interest rates, and creating a budget that prioritizes debt repayment.

Consolidating Debt

Debt consolidation is a popular strategy for managing debt, which involves combining multiple debts into a single loan with a lower interest rate. Consolidating debt can make it easier to manage debt by reducing the number of payments and potentially lowering the total amount of interest paid over time. Here are some steps to take when using debt consolidation to manage debt:

- **Evaluate your debt.**

  Review your debts, including the amounts owed, interest rates, and monthly payments. Evaluating will help you determine whether debt consolidation is a good option.

- **Look for a consolidation loan.**

  There are several types of loans you can use to consolidate your debt, including personal loans, home equity loans, and balance transfer credit cards. Shop around to find the best interest rate and terms for your situation.

- **Apply for the loan.**

  Once you have found a loan that meets your needs, apply for it and provide any required documentation, such as proof of income and credit score.

- **Pay off your debts.**

  Once you receive the loan funds, use them to pay off your existing debts. Doing this will leave you with a single monthly payment on the new loan.

- **Stick to your budget.**

  To avoid accumulating more debt, create a budget that allows you to make your loan payments and covers your living expenses. Stick to your budget and avoid overspending.

- **Avoid accruing new debt.**

  To make the most of your debt consolidation loan, avoid using credit cards or taking out new loans while paying off your debt.

Overall, debt consolidation can be an effective strategy for managing debt, especially if you have multiple high-interest debts. By consolidating your debt into a single loan with a lower interest rate, you can potentially save money and make it easier to manage your debt over time. However, it's important to remember that debt consolidation is not a one-size-fits-all solution and may not be the best option for everyone. Before you determine whether debt consolidation suits, it is crucial to assess the advantages and disadvantages and contemplate alternative debt management tactics.

Negotiate with Creditors

Negotiating with creditors for lower interest rates can be an effective strategy to lower debt, but it requires careful planning and execution. Here are some steps to follow when negotiating with creditors:

- **Gather Information.**

  Before negotiating with creditors, you should gather information about your debt, including the current interest rate, outstanding balance, and payment history. It would help also to research the current market interest rates for similar loans and credit products.

- **Prepare a Proposal.**

  Based on your research, you should prepare a proposal outlining why you need a lower interest rate and how it will benefit you and the creditor. Be specific about how much you will pay and how long you need to repay the debt.

- **Contact the Creditor.**

  You should contact the creditor and explain your situation. Be polite, respectful, and honest about your financial difficulties. Explain how a lower interest rate would help you to repay the debt and maintain a good credit score.

- **Negotiate.**

  The creditor may be willing to negotiate a lower interest rate, especially if you have a good payment history or can provide evidence of financial hardship. Be prepared to discuss the details of your proposal and negotiate the terms of the new interest rate.

- **Get the Agreement in Writing.**

  If you reach an agreement with the creditor, make sure to get the agreement in writing. It will ensure that both parties understand the terms of the new interest rate and prevent any misunderstandings or disputes in the future.

Overall, negotiating with creditors for lower interest rates requires preparation, patience, and effective communication. By following these steps, you can increase your chances of successfully lowering your debt and improving your financial situation.

Creating a Budget

Creating a budget is essential for financial planning and achieving financial goals, such as debt repayment. Here are the steps to create a budget that prioritizes debt repayment:

- **Determine your Income.**

  The first step in creating a budget is to determine how much money you have coming in each month. The budget includes your salary, any side hustle, and any other sources of income.

- **List your Expenses.**

  List all your monthly expenses, including rent/mortgage, utilities, groceries, transportation, entertainment, and other bills. Be sure to include any minimum payments on your debts.

- **Identify Unnecessary Expenses.**

  Review your list of expenses and identify any items that are not essential or that you can reduce, such as dining out, subscription services, or expensive hobbies.

- **Categorize your Expenses.**

  Group your expenses into categories, such as housing, food, transportation, and debt repayment, will help you identify areas to cut back or allocate more funds.

- **Set debt repayment goals.**

  Determine how much debt you want to pay off each month and set a specific goal; will help you stay motivated and focused on reducing your debt.

- **Prioritize debt repayment.**

  Allocate a significant portion of your budget towards debt repayment. If possible, pay more than the minimum amount required to reduce the principal balance and save on interest charges.

- **Review your budget regularly.**

    Review your budget regularly to ensure that you stay on track and make adjustments as needed.

    In summary, creating a budget that prioritizes debt repayment involves:

    1. Identifying your income and expenses.
    2. Categorizing your expenses.
    3. Setting debt repayment goals.
    4. Allocating a significant portion of your budget towards debt repayment.

    By sticking to your budget and making consistent payments towards your debts, you can reduce your debt over time and achieve financial freedom.

Build Good Credit

Building credit is also important in managing debt and achieving financial success. Good credit is essential for accessing loans and other forms of credit, and it can help you get better terms and lower interest rates on your debts. Building credit involves using credit responsibly, paying bills on time, and keeping credit card balances low.

Building good credit involves establishing a track record of responsible borrowing and repayment behavior. Here are some steps you can take to build good credit:

- **Make All Payments on Time.**

  Your payment history is crucial in determining your credit score. Late payments can stay on your credit report for up to seven years and negatively impact your score.

- **Keep Credit Utilization Low.**

  Your credit utilization is the amount of credit you use compared to the amount of credit you have available. It's best to keep this ratio under 30%.

- **Establish Credit.**

  If you're starting out, consider applying for a secured credit card or a credit-builder loan to help establish your credit history.

- **Diversify Credit Mix.**

  A mix of different types of credit (such as credit cards, auto loans, and mortgages) can show lenders that you can handle different types of debt.

- **Monitor Credit Report.**

  Check your credit report regularly to ensure no errors or fraudulent accounts are listed. You can get a free copy of your credit report from each of the three major credit bureaus once a year.

By following these steps and practicing responsible borrowing and repayment behavior, you can build a strong credit history and increase your chances of being approved for credit in the future.

By managing debt and building credit, you can create a robust financial foundation, reduce stress and financial worries, and improve your overall financial well-being. Can help you live with a sense of peace, confidence, and security, knowing that you are in control of your finances and well-prepared for the future.

A young woman named Sarah lived in a small town. She had always been good with money and saved up a decent amount from her job as a waitress. One day, she decided to invest her savings in a small business idea that she had been thinking about for a long time.

Sarah worked hard, her business started growing, and she became quite successful. She was proud of what she had achieved and that she didn't owe anyone any money. However, one day, she realized she needed to expand her business to keep up with the competition. She didn't have enough money to do it, so she decided to take out a loan from a bank.

At first, Sarah was excited about the possibilities the loan would provide. She could expand her business, hire more employees, and increase her profits. However, as time passed, she realized she was now a slave to the bank. She had to make sure she made enough money to repay the loan every month, and she couldn't take any risks that might jeopardize her ability to make the payment.

Sarah constantly worried about the loan and her business and felt like she was no longer in control of her own life. The bank had the power to control her life, and she didn't like it.

Eventually, Sarah paid off her loan and vowed never to borrow money again. She learned that debt-free was more important than having a larger business or more profits. She was happy with her small business and knew she was again in control of her life.

The moral of the story is that borrowing money can be helpful, but it's essential to understand the risks and ensure that you're not putting yourself in a position where you're no longer in control of your own life. As the proverb says, the borrower is the slave of the lender, so it's important to be careful with your finances and to live within your means.

> The rich rule over the poor, and the borrower is slave to the lender. - Proverbs 22:7

Reflections

Have you ever negotiated with creditors for lower interest rates?
If yes, how did it go? If not, would you be willing to try it?

_____

_____

_____

_____

_____

_____

_____

_____

_____

_____

Reflections

How do you feel about debt in general? Does it cause you anxiety or stress?

_____

_____

_____

_____

_____

_____

_____

_____

_____

_____

Chapter 7

Overcoming Financial Stress and Anxiety

Financial stress and anxiety can be debilitating and interfere with our ability to live with peace and contentment. It is important to recognize and understand the sources of financial stress and to take proactive steps to reduce or eliminate them.

Some common sources of financial stress include:

Living Beyond our Means

Spending more than we earn, using credit to fund our lifestyle, and relying on debt to pay for essential expenses. You do not need to keep up with other family members or neighbors. It would help if you focused on yourself rather than everyone else. Once you get your overspending under control, your stress level when it comes will lower.

The consequences of living beyond our means can be far-reaching and affect various aspects of our lives. Here are some ways in which it can impact us:

- **Increased Debt.**

One of the most significant impacts of living beyond our means is the accumulation of debt. The more we spend beyond our income, the more debt we incur the more interest we must pay. This habit can result in a never-ending cycle of debt that can be difficult to break.

- **Financial Stress.**

As the debt increases, so does the financial burden. It can be challenging to manage bills, make ends meet, and deal with the pressure of mounting debt. Financial stress can impact our mental and physical health and relationships.

- **Limited Financial Options.**

Living beyond our means can limit our financial options. We may not have the resources to invest in opportunities to help us grow our wealth or save for emergencies or future expenses. This can limit our financial security and stability.

- **Impaired Credit Score.**

Late payments, missed payments, and high credit card balances can all negatively impact our credit score. A low credit score can limit our ability to get loans or credit in the future. It may result in higher interest rates or unfavorable terms.

- **Strained Relationships.**

  Financial stress can strain our relationships with loved ones. It can be challenging to communicate effectively about money, especially when we feel guilty or embarrassed about our spending habits. This can lead to arguments, tension, and, ultimately, the breakdown of relationships.

  Overall, living beyond our means can significantly impact our lives. Living within our means and practicing good financial habits are vital to avoid the negative consequences of financial stress and debt.

Unpredictable Income

Working in a job with unstable or irregular income or living in an unstable economic environment. Many companies may not have the benefit of vacation pay or personal days. Therefore, if you don't work, you don't get paid. When you are a business owner, if you don't work, you don't make sales and get paid, which can cause high stress for yourself and other family members. Another unpredictable income is the economy. At the time of this writing, the inflation rate is higher than wages. Therefore, when the wages are not keeping up with the cost of living, you spend more on groceries and gas. The money you earn is not going as far as it used to. Once inflation decreases and wages increase, they will meet and come together. Hopefully, the wages will go over the inflation. Therefore, your income will last longer.

Here are some ways in which unpredictable income can impact us:

- **Difficulty Budgeting.**

  Unpredictable income can make creating and sticking to a budget challenging. Without a steady income, it can be tough to determine how much money we can allocate to different expenses and savings goals. This can lead to overspending, which can cause financial stress and make it challenging to meet our financial obligations.

- **Inability to Plan for the Future.**

  Unpredictable income can make it difficult to prepare for the future. It can be challenging to save for retirement, pay for large expenses, or invest in our future when we don't know how much money we will earn. This can lead to feelings of uncertainty and insecurity about our financial future.

- **Increased Debt.**

  Unpredictable income can also lead to increased debt. If we don't have a steady income, we may rely on credit cards or loans to pay for our expenses. This can lead to a cycle of debt that can be difficult to break out of, especially if our income continues to fluctuate.

- **Stress and Anxiety.**

  Unpredictable income can cause significant stress and anxiety. Living with the uncertainty of not knowing how much money we will earn in the future can be challenging. It can be difficult to manage our financial obligations without a steady income can lead to feelings of anxiety, depression, and other mental health issues.

- **Difficulty Qualifying for Loans.**

    Unpredictable income can also make qualifying for loans or credit challenging. Lenders may be hesitant to lend to someone with an irregular income, as they may see them as a higher-risk borrower.

Overall, unpredictable income can have a significant impact on our lives. Therefore, it is crucial to develop strategies to manage this type of financial stress, such as creating a flexible budget to accommodate changes in income and building an emergency fund to help cover unexpected expenses.

Lack of Emergency Savings

Not having enough savings to cover unexpected expenses, such as a medical emergency or job loss. If there is a once-in-a-lifetime pandemic like there was in 2020. Many people were out of work for many months. They lost their homes, vehicles, and more because they had no emergency savings.

Here are some ways in which a lack of emergency savings can impact us:

- **Increased Debt.**

    Without emergency savings, we may rely on credit cards or loans to pay for unexpected expenses or emergencies. Overspending can lead to increased debt, which can be difficult to pay off and cause financial stress.

- **Limited Financial Options.**

  A lack of emergency savings can limit our financial options. We may not have the resources to invest in opportunities to help us grow our wealth or save for future expenses; can limit our financial security and stability.

- **Increased Stress and Anxiety.**

  A lack of emergency savings can cause significant stress and anxiety. Managing unexpected expenses without the financial resources to cover them can be challenging. This can lead to feelings of anxiety, depression, and other mental health issues.

- **Difficulty Achieving Financial Goals.**

  A lack of emergency savings can make it difficult to achieve our financial goals. Without the resources to cover unexpected expenses, we may need to divert funds away from our savings goals, such as saving for a down payment on a house or retirement.

- **Risk of Financial Hardship.**

  A lack of emergency savings can make us vulnerable. Suppose we experience a job loss, medical emergency, or other unexpected expense. In that case, we may need more resources to cover it. leading to a cycle of financial stress and hardship.

Overall, a lack of emergency savings can significantly impact our lives. Building an emergency fund that can help us cover unexpected expenses and emergencies is important. This can help us achieve financial security and stability and reduce the stress and anxiety of financial uncertainty.

Debt

When you owe a significant amount of money, exceptionally high-interest consumer debt such as outstanding credit card balances or personal loans, their debt levels become substantial. This stress can have a significant impact on their lives in several ways:

- **Mental and emotional health:** Financial stress can take a toll on mental and emotional health, leading to anxiety, depression, and other mental health issues. People who are stressed about their finances may struggle to sleep, experience mood swings, and feel overwhelmed by their daily responsibilities.

- **Physical Health.**

  Financial stress can also have a negative impact on physical health. Chronic stress can lead to a weakened immune system, high blood pressure, and other health problems.

- **Relationships.**

  Debt can strain personal relationships, especially if one person is responsible for most of the debt. Arguments about money can be a common source of conflict in relationships. They may lead to feelings of resentment and frustration.

- **Career and Work Performance.**

  Financial stress can also impact career and work performance. When stressed about finances, individuals may have trouble focusing on their work, miss deadlines, or struggle with productivity.

The overall quality of life: Ultimately, financial stress can impact a person's overall quality of life. It can make it challenging to enjoy hobbies or activities and limit personal growth and development opportunities.

Taking proactive measures to manage debt and enhance financial health is imperative to minimize the effects of debt-related financial stress. This might include creating a budget, seeking financial counseling or advice, and exploring debt consolidation or other debt management strategies. Communication with loved ones about financial challenges and working together to find solutions is vital.

Fear Of The Future

Worrying about retirement, health care costs, and other long-term financial obligations.

Here are some ways In which fear of the future can affect our lives:

- **Decision-Making.**

  Fear of the future can make it difficult to make critical financial decisions. When we're worried about what might happen, we may be hesitant to invest in our future or make big purchases, even if necessary.

- **Planning**

  Fear of the future can also make planning difficult in the long term. We may feel like we need to figure out what's going to happen, so we can't make a solid plan for retirement or other major life goals.

- **Saving.**

  When we're worried about the future, we may be less likely to save money. This can lead to a sense of helplessness and a feeling that we don't have control over our financial situation.

- **Stress and Anxiety.**

  Fear of the future can also cause significant stress and anxiety. This can lead to a range of physical and emotional symptoms, including headaches, insomnia, and mood swings.

- **Avoidance.**

  In some cases, fear of the future can lead to avoidance behavior. We may avoid thinking about or dealing with our financial situation because it's too overwhelming, which can lead to even more stress and anxiety over time.

Let me tell you about Matt.

Matt had always been a hardworking man and was proud of his ability to provide for his family. But when his wife, Maria, became ill and was placed in hospice, everything changed.

Matt spent long days by Maria's side, holding her hand and trying to keep her comfortable. But as he watched her condition deteriorate, he became increasingly fearful about how he would be able to pay for her medical bills. He had insurance, of course, but it seemed like every day brought a new expense, medication, and treatment not covered.

At night, when he was alone in their small apartment, Matt would sit at the kitchen table and stare at the pile of bills that seemed to grow bigger every day. He couldn't bear the thought of losing Maria, but he also couldn't bear the idea of being left with nothing.

One evening, as he sat at the table with tears streaming down his face, Matt heard a knock at the door. It was his neighbor, Mrs. Johnson, an elderly woman who had always been kind to him and Maria.

"Matt, I heard you were crying, and I came to see if everything was okay," she said gently.

Matt didn't want to burden her with his problems, but something about her kind presence made him want to open up. So, he told her about Maria's illness, the mounting bills, and his fear of losing everything.

Mrs. Johnson listened patiently, and when he finished, she took his hand and looked him in the eye.

"Matt, I know this is hard. But you are not alone. You have friends who care about you, and you have a strength inside you that you don't even know about yet. You will get through this and become stronger on the other side."

Her words were like a balm to Matt's soul. For the first time in weeks, he felt a glimmer of hope.

Over the next few days, Matt started to take action. He contacted a financial advisor who helped him navigate the complicated world of medical bills and insurance. He reached out to friends and family who offered to help in any way they could. And he started to see that he did have a strength inside him that he could rely on.

Maria passed away a few weeks later, and Matt felt a profound sense of loss. But he was also left with something else: a newfound appreciation for the people in his life and an understanding of gratitude for the small things that made life worth living.

Years later, when Matt looked back on that difficult time, he knew it had changed him in ways he could never have imagined. And he knew that he had Mrs. Johnson to thank for showing him that there is always hope, even in the darkest times.

Taking proactive measures to prepare for unexpected events is crucial to alleviate financial stress stemming from apprehension regarding the future. This might include building an emergency fund, investing in insurance or other forms of protection, and seeking advice from financial experts or mentors. It's also helpful to focus on the present moment and take steps to address immediate financial challenges rather than getting too caught up in worries about the future.

Adopting a comprehensive and proactive approach to managing finances is crucial in conquering financial anxiety and stress. This may involve creating a budget, reducing spending, increasing savings, and seeking professional financial advice.

It is also vital to take steps to manage stress and anxiety in general, such as practicing mindfulness, engaging in physical exercise, seeking social support, and focusing on gratitude and positive thoughts.

Combining financial savvy with self-care and stress management can create a sense of financial peace and security, reduce stress and anxiety, and live with greater well-being and joy. This can help you to be more focused, productive, and confident in all areas of your life, including your spiritual growth and relationship with God.

Do not be anxious about anything, but in every situation, by prayer and petition, with thanksgiving, present your requests to God. And the peace of God, which transcends all understanding, will guard your hearts and your minds in Christ Jesus. - Philippians 4:6-7

Reflections

What financial habits have you adopted that contribute to financial stress?

_____

_____

_____

_____

_____

_____

_____

_____

_____

_____

Reflections

What steps can you take to reduce financial stress in your life?

_____

_____

_____

_____

_____

_____

_____

_____

_____

_____

_____

A big part of financial freedom is having your heart and mind free from worry about the what ifs of life.

Suze Orman, Financial Author

Chapter 8

How to Find Inner Peace
in a Material World

Wealth and material success can bring many benefits. Still, they can also create stress and anxiety and interfere with our spiritual growth and well-being. It is crucial to understand the spiritual aspect of wealth and to cultivate a healthy relationship with money and material success, to find inner peace and happiness. Several of us have a complex relationship with money, involving love and hate. Sometimes it is hard to find peace in a material world. We must learn to be content where we are but continue moving forward.

Here are some key principles to keep in mind:

Money is a Tool, Not an End in Itself

Money can be a valuable resource that enables us to achieve our goals, but it should never be the primary focus of our lives. Think about money as a tool in your toolkit. It would be best to have it, but you must ensure you use it wisely.

For example, an 8-year-old boy named Timmy. He loved candy more than anything in the world. One day, Timmy got his hands on a candy cane wrapped so tightly that he couldn't open it with his bare hands.

He was determined to get to his candy, so he went to my toolbox and found a power drill. He thought it was the perfect tool for the job and started drilling into the candy wrapper with all his might.

But despite all his efforts, the candy wrapper remained stubbornly sealed shut. He got frustrated and decided to try a different approach. He rummaged through the toolbox and found a pair of pliers, which he thought would do the trick.

Timmy used the pliers to grip the edge of the candy wrapper and pulled with all his might. But to his dismay, the candy wrapper still refused to budge.

When Timmy was about to give up and cry, his big brother walked in and asked what he was doing. Timmy explained his predicament, and his brother laughed and told him he was using the wrong tool for the job.

His brother then grabbed a pair of scissors and snipped open the candy wrapper in two seconds flat. Timmy was relieved. He realized he had been using the wrong tools and couldn't help but laugh at his silly mistake.

From then on, Timmy made sure to use the right tool for the job, and he never had any trouble opening his candy again. And every time he saw that power drill in my toolbox, he couldn't help but chuckle and remember his funny little mishap.

True Wealth is Not Just Financial

Wealth is about much more than just money. It encompasses physical, emotional, social, and spiritual well-being. True wealth refers to a state of holistic abundance that goes beyond mere financial prosperity. These aspects of wealth are interconnected and interdependent. A person possessing all these aspects of wealth can live a fulfilling and satisfying life.

- **Physical Well-Being.**

  It encompasses being in good health, having enough energy to do what one wants to do, and having the ability to engage in physical activities. Good physical health can help prevent chronic diseases, such as heart disease, diabetes, and cancer, which can be expensive to treat. Exercise is one way to maintain physical health, and it can also promote emotional well-being. Eating a healthy diet is vital for physical well-being.

- **Emotional Well-Being**.

  It refers to a state of inner peace and contentment, free from anxiety, stress, and negative emotions. Mindfulness practices, therapy, and positive social relationships can cultivate emotional well-being. For example, spending time with loved ones or engaging in activities that bring joy can boost emotional well-being.

- **Social Well-Being**.

  Involves having a sense of belonging, being part of a community, and having positive relationships with others. Social connections can be a source of support during difficult times and can contribute to overall well-being. Examples of activities promoting social well-being include volunteering, joining a community group or club, or simply spending time with friends.

- **Spiritual Well-Being**.

  Refers to a sense of purpose, meaning, and connection to something greater than oneself. This can involve religious or spiritual practices, meditation, or connecting with nature. Spiritual well-being can provide a sense of inner peace and a source of strength during challenging times.

In conclusion, true wealth encompasses physical, emotional, social, and spiritual well-being. By focusing on all these aspects of wealth, we can live a fulfilling and satisfying life. Actions promoting true wealth include exercise, healthy eating, mindfulness practices, positive social relationships, volunteering, and spiritual practices.

Gratitude and Contentment are Key

Being grateful for what we have and content with our circumstances, rather than constantly striving for more, can bring great peace and happiness. Being thankful for what you have can promote health, happiness, and success. Being content where you are means you stay content in the situation until the situation changes. It's not necessary to go out and buy stuff to make you feel better gratitude is the platform where hope arises. Looking at what you have and thanking God for what you have will give you inner peace, and you'll be happy. Robert A. Evans and Michael E McCullough were with the research project on gratitude and thankfulness. They commented that grateful people report higher levels of positive emotions, laugh satisfaction, vitality optimism, and lower levels of depression and stress the disposition toward gratitude appears to enhance pleasant feeling states more than it diminishes unpleasant emotions.

Generosity and Kindness are Important

Giving our time, talents, and resources can bring great joy and fulfillment and deepen our spiritual connection with others. Generosity is also a state of mind. Generosity is when you want to give and help others is when wealth begins. When you start to serve, giving money and time to help others allows you to stay in perspective with what you have. You don't have to wait until you become rich; start now. Keep a little; you give what you can, whether you give a little money or time. Engage in random acts of generosity.

Being spontaneous is something you can see when helping somebody else. Random acts of generosity can also be acts of kindness. Look at somebody straight in the face, straight in the eyeballs, and say I see you. Have a good day. May God bless you. When somebody knows that you see them for who they are, that gives them more self-worth.

Seek Balance

Striving for financial success can be a positive and productive pursuit, but it should never consume our lives. It is important to seek balance and make time for other important aspects of life, such as relationships, health, and spiritual growth.

Therefore, making time for these aspects of life is crucial to ensure we live a balanced and fulfilling life.

- **Relationships.**

  They are an essential aspect of life and investing time and effort into them. Building and maintaining healthy relationships with family, friends, and partners can provide a sense of connection and support and contribute to overall well-being. For example, taking the time to have regular family dinners, scheduling regular dates with a partner, or making time to catch up with friends can help strengthen these relationships.

- **Health**.

  It's essential to prioritize it. Taking care of our physical and mental health can help us function at our best and provide a foundation for achieving our goals. For example, exercising, eating a healthy diet, getting enough sleep, and taking care of our mental health through meditation or therapy can all contribute to overall well-being.

- **Spiritual Growth.**

  It is essential to be available for it. Whether through religious or spiritual practices, connecting with nature, or simply taking time for self-reflection, nurturing our spiritual well-being can provide a sense of purpose and meaning in life. For example, attending religious services, going on a nature walk, or journaling can all be ways to foster spiritual growth.

In conclusion, achieving balance means making time for all aspects of life, including relationships, health, and spiritual growth. By prioritizing these areas, we can lead fulfilling and well-rounded lives. Examples of actions that can help us achieve balance include:

- Scheduling regular time for family and friends.
- Making time for exercise and healthy eating.
- Engaging in practices that nurture our spiritual well-being.

By incorporating these spiritual principles into our relationship with money and wealth, we can find greater inner peace and happiness and live a more fulfilling and meaningful life.

"Do not store up for yourselves treasures on earth, where moths and vermin destroy, and where thieves break in and steal. But store up for yourselves treasures in heaven, where moths and vermin do not destroy, and where thieves do not break in and steal. For where your treasure is, there your heart will be also.

- Matthew 6:19-21

Reflections

What is your current relationship with money, and how does it affect your spiritual well-being?

_____

_____

_____

_____

_____

_____

_____

_____

_____

_____

Reflections

Describe a time when you felt a deep sense of purpose or connection to something greater than yourself. What did it feel like, and how did it affect you?

_____

_____

_____

_____

_____

_____

_____

_____

_____

_____

_____

_____

Chapter 9

Prioritizing Wellness and Happiness

So now you're thinking, how can I get a balanced life in the world? Everyone desires something that requires constant attention and maintenance. How do I balance?

Dangers of Burnout and Stress and How to Manage Them Effectively

Burnout and stress can significantly negatively impact our physical and mental health. When we experience chronic stress, it can lead to feelings of exhaustion, cynicism, and reduced efficacy, which are the hallmarks of burnout. : Burnout can cause us to feel emotionally drained, irritable, and overwhelmed. It can even lead to physical health problems such as headaches, digestive issues, and chronic pain.

Regarding managing burnout and stress effectively, it is essential to prioritize self-care and take steps to reduce stress levels. Here are a few strategies that can be helpful:

- **Identify Sources of Stress.**

  One of the first steps in managing burnout and stress is to identify what is causing it. Consider making a list of the things that cause stress and burnout in your life. This list can help you identify patterns and develop strategies to manage them effectively.

- **Practice Self-Care.**

  Self-care is critical for managing stress and preventing burnout. It may include exercise, meditation, yoga, getting enough sleep, and eating a healthy diet. Take time to prioritize self-care in your daily routine.

We can get burned out when we do not ask for help. When it comes to doing a task, I have seen this repeatedly with family and friends that get so burnt out that they want to stop doing everything. They want people to leave them alone, and then the depression hits, and they have no clue why they feel the way they do. Sometimes, you need to step back, take a break, take a vacation, or go on a road trip. Even if it's just for 24 to 48 hours, it will relieve the stress because there are times you have to ask for help to make it through this period, and taking time off is essential.

Here is an example:

One day, a burnt-out employee went to work and found herself unable to complete even the simplest tasks. She was so overwhelmed by stress and exhaustion that she couldn't focus on anything and felt like she was on the verge of a breakdown.

In an effort to distract herself from her stress, she decided to take a break and make a cup of tea. She filled the kettle with water, turned on the stove, and sat at her desk to wait.

After a few minutes, she realized she had completely forgotten about the kettle and the boiling water on the stove. So, she rushed to the kitchen, only to find that the water had boiled away, and the kettle was now smoking and ruined.

Frustrated and defeated, she sat at her desk and burst into tears. Her co-workers rushed to her side to see what was wrong, only to find her sobbing over a ruined kettle.

While this story may seem silly, it highlights how burnout can affect our ability to focus and complete even the most straightforward tasks. Taking breaks and prioritizing self-care is essential to avoid burnout and maintain well-being.

Set Boundaries

Learning to say "no" and setting boundaries is essential for preventing burnout. Know your limits and recognize when to take a break or say no to additional commitments. Many Americans work all the time, mainly because of technology. You get a phone call from your supervisor, and you feel like you have to answer it, and it doesn't matter if it's within your eight-to-five job or not. You are on call 24/7 and must learn to set boundaries. Trust me when I say this, people will not like it when you set boundaries. Learn to say no. It's okay. Put your phone on, do not disturb, when fulfilling your personal needs. You do not have to answer the phone every time it rings.

You can wait to answer a text and do not have to respond immediately. The constant notifications from our devices have made us feel constantly engaged and distracted. Focusing on your goals and tasks can be challenging when your phone continually rings with calls from people needing your attention. Establishing boundaries by taking breaks from daily routines and disconnecting from your phone is essential. Learning to say "no" is also crucial in managing your time effectively and controlling your schedule. I did this not too long ago when I received a text at 6:30 in the morning. Well, at that time, it should not be about work. I reserve this time for my immediate family, close friends, and no one else.

My immediate family and close friends understand the boundaries of texting or calling too early in the morning. It was when it was early; I first thought something was wrong.

Build a Support System

Having a support system in place can help you manage stress and burnout. Reach out to friends and family for support, consider joining a support group or therapy, and make time for meaningful connections with others. We all need a support system to help us get through this beautiful world we call life or, better yet, the journey of life. When looking for someone to be part of that support system, be sure they will not add to your stress levels. Find this support system that will listen to you and be willing to give you advice when you ask for it. Find the support system that you can laugh with and joke with without any worries of it coming back against you, finding the right people to hang out with that can encourage you and not further stress you out.

Finding the right support system can be crucial for our mental and emotional well-being, as it can provide us with a sense of community, comfort, and validation. Here are some tips on how to find the right support system:

- **Identify Your Needs.**

  Start by thinking about what you need from a support system. Are you looking for someone to listen to you without judgment, someone who can offer practical advice, or someone who can provide emotional support? Knowing what you need can help you find the right group of support systems.

- **Reach Out to Friends and Family.**

  Don't be afraid to reach out to people you feel close to and trust in your existing social network. These may be friends, family members, or co-workers with whom you feel comfortable talking.

- **Join a Support Group.**

  Many support groups are available for various issues and challenges, from mental health to addiction and beyond. Consider searching online or asking your doctor or therapist for recommendations.

- **Find a Therapist or counselor.**

  A mental health professional can provide a safe and confidential space to discuss your feelings and challenges. They can also offer guidance and support to help you manage your mental health.

- **Seek Out Online Communities.**

  There are many online communities and forums where you can connect with others going through similar experiences. These communities can be a great source of information, validation, and support.

When looking for the right support system, it's important to be patient and persistent. Not every person or group will be the right fit, so it's important to keep trying until you find the right fit for you.

Remember, seeking support is a sign of strength, and can be an essential part of your journey toward better mental and emotional health.

Practice Stress-Reducing Techniques

Many techniques can help you manage stress, including deep breathing, progressive muscle relaxation, guided imagery, and mindfulness meditation. Consider trying different approaches to find what works best for you. Here are some things you can consider.

- **5-10 Breathing Exercise.**

  This exercise consists of breathing in five counts and out ten counts. You may be so tense that exhaling for a total count of ten could be challenging. You must continue breathing in five and out ten until breathing slows down. It will lower stress it will lower your blood pressure. Placing your hand over your heart as you breathe will help you know you are okay, and well. Continue breathing until your breaths have come evenly, then your heart rate will decrease, which means your blood pressure has reduced. At this point, continue with what you were doing.

- **Tapping.**

  The tapping method is where you tap on the side of your hand around your little finger. Be consistent in the tapping, not too fast or too slow. If you're at the stress level, you may tap too quickly, but as you tap, you will start lowering your stress level. It will become slower and more even. Acknowledge what is stressing you out. Acknowledging the stress will help you recognize what is causing the stress. When that trigger happens again, you know immediately to go ahead and start into the technique, acknowledge it, and then tell yourself that everything is safe and well. Tapping method, you can also do it on the top of your head. If you have prepared a presentation for your work and anxiety has come over you, you can tell yourself, say, "I'm excited" instead of, "I'm scared." Being excited and fearful are the same feelings, so turn the negative of anxiety and fear into positive excitement; I'm looking forward to this. It will not only change your outward appearance, but you will be able to go in with more confidence with your presentation.

- **5-second Rule.**

  This rule was created by Mel Robbins. It's based on the idea that when you have an impulse to do something, you only have a few seconds before your brain kicks in with doubt, fear, and negative self-talk that can hold you back. So you count down 5, 4, 3, 2, 1, and then take action. The counting down process helps you to interrupt the habit loop of overthinking and second-guessing yourself, and instead, it initiates action.

- **Meditation.**

  Meditating can be prayer and meditation on God's word. Hence, as you're meditating, speak scripture verses just as Jesus did in the desert when the devil genuinely tempted him. Know the scriptures and turn around and say it right back; that will help you know everything is okay.

Take Breaks

Taking breaks throughout the day is essential to recharge and prevent burnout. Taking breaks throughout the day will help you stay focused. When you become so absorbed in your work that you lose the ability to concentrate, it is a sign that you should take a break. Consider taking a short walk, stretching, drinking water, coffee, or a glass of tea and a snack, or taking a power nap.

By prioritizing self-care, setting boundaries, building a support system, and practicing stress-reducing techniques, it is possible to manage burnout and stress effectively. These strategies can help reduce stress levels, prevent burnout, and promote physical and mental well-being.

There is a time for everything, and a season for every activity under the heavens: a time to be born and a time to die, a time to plant and a time to uproot, a time to kill and a time to heal, a time to tear down and a time to build, a time to weep and a time to laugh, a time to mourn and a time to dance, a time to scatter stones and a time to gather them, a time to embrace and a time to refrain from embracing, a time to search and a time to give up, a time to keep and a time to throw away, a time to tear and a time to mend, a time to be silent and a time to speak, a time to love and a time to hate a time for war and a time for peace. - Ecclesiastes 3:1-8

Reflections

What is causing stress and burnout in your life?

_____

_____

_____

_____

_____

_____

_____

_____

_____

_____

_____

Reflections

What are some techniques you have used to manage stress in the past, and what are some new ones you can try?

_____

_____

_____

_____

_____

_____

_____

_____

_____

_____

_____

Wealth is the ability to fully experience life.

Henry David Thoreau

Chapter 10

The Path to Sustainable Prosperity and Inner Peace

The path to sustainable prosperity and inner peace is a journey that requires intention, discipline, and self-awareness. By achieving financial stability, prioritizing wellness and happiness, and cultivating a spiritual perspective, we can find the balance and harmony that lead to lasting peace and prosperity.

We must start by setting achievable financial goals and prioritizing our values. This involves creating a roadmap to prosperity by identifying our financial priorities and making conscious choices with our money. Mindful spending is a vital aspect of this. It consists of being aware of our impact on others and the world around us, and choosing products and services produced responsibly and sustainably.

Overcoming financial stress and anxiety is also essential to achieving inner peace. By managing debt, building credit, and developing a solid financial foundation through savings and investment, we can reduce financial stress and increase our sense of security.

In addition, taking care of our mental and physical well-being is crucial to our overall wellness and happiness. This involves setting boundaries, finding a support system, and making time for leisure and recreation. It is also important to approach life with a spiritual perspective, seeking inner peace and fulfillment through a connection to a higher power.

As we pursue the path to sustainable prosperity and inner peace, we must remember that it is not a destination but a continual journey. We must remain open to growth and change and be willing to adapt our priorities and goals as we evolve. We can find the balance and harmony that lead to a fulfilling and prosperous life with dedication and perseverance.

> I can do all this through him who gives me strength.
> - Philippians 4:13

Notes:

---

[i] (Source: Board of Governors of the Federal Reserve System. (2021). Report on the Economic Well-Being of U.S. Households in 2020 - May 2021. Retrieved from www.federalreserve.gov/publications/2021-economic-well-being-of-us-households-in-2020-executive-summary.htm#_ftnref8.)

www.ingramcontent.com/pod-product-compliance
Lightning Source LLC
Chambersburg PA
CBHW070410220526
45467CB00001B/523